Marketing Strategy
Planning Tool

Karen Porter

$\mathcal{K}$ae Ceative Solutions

P. O. Box 2011

Friendswood, Texas 77549

281-797-3920

kaeporter@gmail.com

Welcome to the

Marketing Strategy Planning Tool

from

ƙae Creative Solutions.

This booklet is a working tool for you to use to define and focus your attention on the marketing strategy that is best for you and your ministry.

The questions are designed to help you discover your strengths and abilities as well as your preferences and inclinations.

There are no right or wrong answers. Instead, as you answer the questions, consider whatever possibilities come to your mind. Every idea and thought is important.

Use your answers to develop promotional tools and your marketing plan. You can work on your own or if you'd like to talk to one of our experienced professionals, please connect with us at ƙae Creative Solutions. We will help you design a marketing strategy that is custom made for you. See our website at www.kaecreative solutions. com for a current price list for evaluation and anaylsis as well as plan development.

We look forward to hearing from you.

Karen Porter

ƙae Creative Solutions

Email: kaeporter@gmail.com

Notes and Additional Information

Name: _____

Address: _____

City/State/Zip _____

Phone _____

Email _____

Website _____

Blog _____

Tell me about your family, marital status, children.

Tell me about places you have lived and any interesting facts about those places or why you lived there.

What church do you belong to? _____

Did you grow up in that denomination?   Yes   No

Would you consider yourself conservative or   liberal? (circle one)

What is your primary personality type?*
 Choleric   Sanguine   Melancholy   Phlegmatic

What is your secondary personality type?*
Choleric   Sanguine   Melancholy   Phlegmatic

*If you haven't taken a personality profile, email kaeporter@gmail.com and we will provide the questionnaire.

Notes and Additional Information

Using the categories below, list where you have spoken or taught before.

TEACHING SPEAKING

BIBLE STUDIES OR TOPICAL

Home Church

Churches other than home church

Subjects taught

Type of group

SCHOOL

Subjects

Ages

COMMUNITY ORGANIZATIONS

Subjects

Ages

Type of Group

OTHER: (Use the opposite page if you need more space.)

Groups/Subjects:

Type of Event:

Type of Group:

Size of Group:

Paid?

How many times have you spoken or taught in the past 12 months?_____

Notes and Additional Information

Writing Experience:

What have you written?

ARTICLES:

Subject

Length

Published? (if so, where/when?)

BOOKS:

Title

Genre

Published? (if so, what publisher and when?)

OTHER:

Notes and Additional Information

Personal Work Characteristics
(Comment on each of the following statements.)

I am a perfectionist.

I procrastinate.

I do not plan ahead.

I have bursts of creative activity.

I like to think through everything before I act.

I start projects but never finish them.

I am a finisher; when I have a plan, I follow it through to the end.

I often start things without considering how much money will be needed.

I set unrealistic deadlines.

I give myself too much time and lose interest

I don't feel I have the tools or expertise I need.

I am often sidetracked with emergencies and unplanned events.

I have a lot of personal commitments right now and don't know when I'll have time to do marketing for my ministry.

My busy time of the year is

I am organized and precise in my commitments.

I keep my calendar up to date.

My calendar is a stack of torn pages and scrap napkins.

I am creative with color, design, graphics.

My hobbies include:

I like:

I hate:

Notes and Additional Information

BUILDING A STRATEGY

<u>SWOT</u>

Strengths: (What are your personal assets, qualities, attributes, talents, and abilities?)

Weaknesses: (What are your personal weak spots, limitations, disadvantages, or flaws?)

Opportunities: (What external conditions in society, culture, churches, communities, might be helpful for your message or marketing plans?)

Threats: (What external conditions in finance, religion, traditions, family life, schedules might do damage to your message or marketing plans?)

Do your best work on these questions as they are vital to developing a marketing strategy.

Notes and Additional Information

PASSION

Describe your viewpoint of the value of each of the following areas:

Family

Marriage

Art

Music

The Bible

Bible Study

Personal Quiet Time

Fun Activities

Work

Vacation

Notes and Additional Information

What is the one subject you feel is most important for Christians to grasp?

Do you think Christians have a handle on this subject? Why or why not?

What is your message on this subject? (give bullet points or outline or a descriptive paragraph)

Notes and Additional Information

AUDIENCE

Who is your target audience?

What is his or her age? (range)

What does he or she like?

What does he or she dislike?

What does he or she worry about?

What does he or she do for fun?

What does he think he needs?

What does she really need?

What messages is he or she getting from the news?

What messages is he or she getting from TV programs?

What messages is he or she getting from media and commercials?

Notes and Additional Information

What messages is he or she getting from his or her peers?

What demands come from his or her work place?

What demands come from nearest family?

What demands come from extended family?

Write a paragraph describing a person in your audience.

Example: My typical audience member is a 40-year-old woman who works hard at her career and family. She worries about her children. She is consumed with juggling finances. She never pampers herself. She never has enough time. She loves the Lord deeply, but wonders if she is following His will and if she is doing anything that has a lasting legacy or has an impact on her world.

Notes and Additional Information

WHAT DO I HAVE TO OFFER?

Circle all of the following words that describe you. Then ask a friend or family member to circle the words they feel would describe you (in a different color ink)

Strong Message	Practical	Comforting	Expertise
Courage	Significant	Useful	Guiding
Reassures	Hope	Skilled	Knowledgeable
Valuable	Encouraging	Accomplished	Cheerful
Competent	Competitive	Creative	Decisive
Dedicated	Eager	Efficient	Determined
Dependable	Enthusiastic	Flexible	Inflexible
Great attitude	Follows through	Listens	Helpful
Interested	Story Teller	Loyal	Patient
Professional	Quick	Reliable	Smart
Strong	Thoughtful	Versatile	Eloquent
Responsive	Accessible	Visionary	Intelligent
Funny	Authoritative	Calm	Flighty
Entertaining	Serious	Animated	Sure

List your top three speaking messages with a one or two sentence description of each one.

1.

2.

3.

Notes and Additional Information

What do your messages offer to listeners/readers?

What has happened to you that makes you able to give your message?

Why does someone need to hear your message?

What other books or speakers offer the same kind of message?

How are you different?

What can you offer that is unique to you?

What about today's culture/society makes your message urgent?

What does your message offer the hearer?

How can your message help the hearer?

How can you serve the hearer of your message?

Notes and Additional Information

Have you produced any of the following about your message?

Handbooks

Guidebooks

Bible studies

Tip Sheets

Other materials

Have you written a book or a book proposal? If so, describe the book and its message. If not, what would you like to write about?

Notes and Additional Information

What three key words describe you?

What font is most descriptive of you, your style, your message?
(check out fonts.com; dafont.com; 1001freefonts.com for ideas)

What colors/color combinations do you like most?

Which of the styles below describes how you would like your marketing materials to look?

Sophisticated	Cute	Modern	Humorous
Geometric	Flowery	Colorful	Academic
Professional	Feminine	Classic	Romantic
Edgy	Bold	Clean	Old World

Other: _____

Notes and Additional Information

In each of the categories below, describe your relative strength or weakness and your unique message in the category if any.

Doctrine

Ethics

Perspective

Social Issues

Principles

Encouragement

Instructions

Guidelines

Practical helps

Counseling

Notes and Additional Information

What books have you read in the last 3 years?

What books or speakers influenced you and your message?

Is there any speaker that you feel you are like? Or very unlike?

What conferences have you attended? What did you gain or fail to gain from each one?

Notes and Additional Information

If you have written a Mission Statement, please write it below. If you have not written one, write three or four words that describe your mission.

Definition: A mission statement describes your overall ministry. It is used like an umbrella or a filter to help you make decisions about what you will and won't do in choosing your priorities. It is the focus and foundation of your whole ministry. It expresses the highest ideals and is deeper than a money objective. It is the verbal equivalent of "reaching for the stars" It is God's call on your life. It will sound great and lofty; it is suppose to! It can be long or short.

If you have written a TAG LINE, please write it below.

Definition: A tag line is a zippy sound bite. It is very simple and very positive. It may fit only the current message/book/speech/project. It will be short.

Notes and Additional Information

VALUE STATEMENTS:

List at least 3 statements that describe the VALUE that you bring to your audience (in either speaking or writing)

Definition: Value statements express the principles or standards that you offer your audience. Ask yourself: how will what I have to say help them?

1.

2.

3.

BRAND:

If you have given thought to a brand idea, discuss it here. If not, we will begin building your brand in our face-to-face sessions.

Definition: A brand reflects your unique style….especially in content, category, and characterization.

Notes and Additional Information

WEBSITE:

Do you have a website?

URL: _____

Did you have a professional build it? _____

Can you change information on the page yourself? _____

Do you change information on the page often?_____

Does your current website reflect the image you want to project?

BLOG

Do you have a blog?

Address: _____-

How often do you blog? _____

Do you get comments on your blogs?_____

If so, how many per blog? _____

Notes and Additional Information

What are your hobbies or activities or interests that are not part of your current message/books/writings/speeches?

Do you have expertise in any of the following?

Meal Planning	Music
Organizing	Water Color
Cleaning tips	Car mechanics for women
Saving $	Calligraphy
Raising Kids	Exercise for busy moms
Adoption	Collecting
Doing Laundry	Dancing
Giving Kids Birthday Parties	Cooking
Hunting or Fishing	Frozen Meals
Camping	Antiques (refinishing)
Traveling	Garage Sale tips
A way to remember birthdays	Kitchen Gadgets
Scrapbooking	Ceramics
Jewelry Making	Photograph
Sewing	Quilting
Crafts	Other:_____

Notes and Additional Information

Are you on Facebook?

How often do you post?

How many friends does your page have?

Do you Twitter?

How often do you post?

How many are you following?

How many follow you?

Are you on Instagram?

How often do you post?

What type pictures do you post?

Do you have a newsletter?

Do you send it by mail or email?

How many on your distribution list?

What service do you use to post your newsletter?

Do you have a mailing list? Snail mail? Email?

Have you had professional photos made?

When?

Notes and Additional Information

Have you produced any of the following?

One sheet

Business Cards

Any Promotional materials (postcards, book marks, etc)

Photos

CD/DVD

Endorsements

Statement of Faith

Copy of latest newsletter if any

Printout of latest blog, if any

Any other promotional materials you have already produced.

If not, begin to create each of these items using what you've learned about yourself in this marketing strategy tool. What words, colors, fonts, styles would you prefer?

If you choose to have a one-on-one meeting by phone or in person with one of our specialists, bring or send these materials.

Notes and Additional Information

ASSETS/TOOLS: *Do you have connections with people who could help you with or you could hire for the following services:*

Graphic artist

Photographer

Web designer

Printer

Friends on the Internet

Video

Recording

TV

Local businesses (book stores)

Email

Church

Denominations

National Organizations

National Conventions

Other: _____

Notes and Additional Information

Financial: *(As you develop your marketing plan, count the costs.*

Costs

Office:

      Equipment (computers, printers, etc. $_____

      Supplies $_____

      Assistant $_____

Media Kit: $_____

Business Cards $_____

Letterhead $_____

Fliers $_____

Outside Marketing Firm $_____

Seminars and training $_____

Other: $_____

TOTAL

Revenue Sources:

Savings

Seed Money to Begin

Personal Investments

Outside Investors

Loans/Grants, etc.

My financial resources are a total of $_____

I am willing to invest $_____ per month in marketing my ministry.

ƙae Creative Solutions

Where Your Future Looks Bright

www.kaecreativesolutions.com

ƙae Creative Solutions is a communications consulting firm. Our goal is to coach you to excellence in your writing, speaking, and marketing. Our team of experienced professionals will help you become the best in your field.

Your career or ministry success may depend on your coach.

We have proven methods for building a platform and getting your book, message, or idea noticed.

We Coach Speakers

- Presentation Analysis
- Content Development
- Voice Coaching
- Story-telling
- Humor
- Style Critique
- Constructive / Practical Helps

We Coach Writers

- Content Editing

- Line Proofing

- Overall Concept Analysis

- Ghost Writing

- Book Doctoring

- Book Production Services

- Cover Design

We Coach Marketing

- Marketing Plan Development

- Tag Line Development

- Graphic Artist Services

- Pitch and Advertising Coaching

- Promotional Materials

- Branding

In addition to our all-star team, founder Karen Porter will take a personal interest in your wrirting, speaking, and marketing.

*k*ae Creative Solutions

PO Box 2011

Friendswood, Texas 77549

Email: kaeporter@gmail.com